FIRST
PAINT
Activity
BOOK

Dawn Sirett

DK Publishing

Previously published as *My First Paint Book*

DK

LONDON, NEW YORK, MUNICH,
MELBOURNE, and DELHI

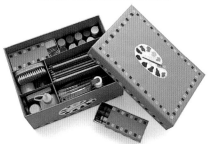

Art editor Mandy Earey
Photography Dave King
Senior designer Neville Graham
Senior editors Marie Greenwood,
Sue Nicholson
Production Amy Bennett

DK Delhi
Senior editor Glenda Fernandes
Senior designer Shefali Upadhyay
Designer Mini Dhawan
DTP designer Harish Aggarwal

First American Edition published in 1994
under the title *My First Paint Book*
This edition published in the United States in 2007 by
DK Publishing
375 Hudson Street
New York, New York 10014

07 08 09 10 10 9 8 7 6 5 4 3 2 1
MD370 - 10/06

A catalog record for this book is available from
the Library of Congress.

ISBN 978-0-7566-2580-1

Reproduced by Media Development
and Printing Ltd, UK
Printed and bound by Leo Paper Products Ltd, China

Discover more at
www.dk.com

2

CONTENTS

3

PAINTING BY PICTURES

First Paint Activity Book shows you how to make and paint all kinds of wonderful things using everyday materials. Step-by-step photographs and simple instructions tell you exactly what you do, and there are photographs of all the finished projects. At the end of the book, you'll find some craft paper and a pattern for the gift bag shown on page 12.

How to use this book

What the project is about
The introduction to each project tells you important information about the activity shown.

Equipment
Illustration checklists show you which tools you will need to have ready before you start each project.

The materials you need
The items for each project are shown clearly to help you check that you have everything you need.

PERFECT PRINTS

Printing is a fun way to use paint and the results look great. Thick, sticky paint works best. All kinds of things such as cardboard, vegetables, or even your fingers can be used as printing tools. A sponge on an old cookie sheet makes a good printing pad. To keep from mixing colors, use one tool for each color and let the first color dry when printing one color over another.

EQUIPMENT
Sharp knife
Scissors
Cookie sheet
Household sponges
Jar of water

You will need

Writing paper
Poster paints
Printing tools
Paintbrush
Small matchbox
Button
Large and small carrots
A piece of thin household sponge
Cotton swab
Large and small cardboard tubes
Plastic drinking straw
Envelopes
Thick cardboard
Ridged cardboard

PRINTING THE PAPER

The finished prints
Try printing a border, a stamp mark, or a picture on the paper and envelopes. Make sure you leave space to write in!

Ground printed with the edge of ridged cardboard

Tree prints made with a sponge and the edge of cardboard

Circle print made with a cardboard tube

Pattern printed with a button and a small tube

Border printed with a triangular sponge

Circle prints made with a cotton swab and a straw

Put some damp sponges on an old cookie sheet. Pour paint and a little water on to the sponges*. Spread out the paint with a brush.

Ask an adult to cut the carrots. Cut a sponge shape. Press each tool into the paint and place firmly on paper to make a print**.

Print with different colors and tools to make a pattern or picture on the paper. Put more paint on each tool every few prints.

Tractor printed with carrots, a matchbox, the edge of cardboard, and a cotton swab

*The paint needs to be thick and sticky.
**Practice on scrap paper first.

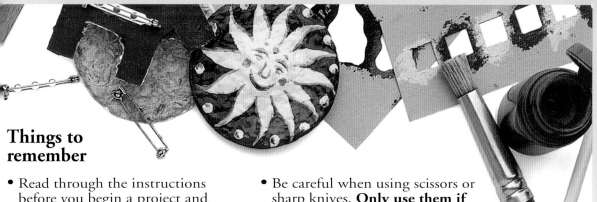

Things to remember

- Read through the instructions before you begin a project and gather together everything you will need.
- Put on an apron or old shirt before you start and roll up your sleeves.
- Lay down lots of newspaper to protect work tables and the floor.

- Be careful when using scissors or sharp knives. **Only use them if an adult is there to help you**.
- Always open the windows when using oil-based varnish and ask an adult to clean the brush in paint thinner for you.
- Put everything away when you have finished and clean up any mess.

Step-by-step
Step-by-step photographs and clear instructions tell you exactly what to do at each stage of a project.

Painting tips
Look out for useful tips, which give you extra information about a painting technique.

The finished project
Photographs show you what the finished projects look like, making it easy to copy them.

PAINTED BOTTLES

Try turning empty bottles or jars into pretty vases and pots. Clean and dry the bottles or jars before painting them. Be careful with glass: keep the bottle or jar on a table while painting it. Finish with a coat of varnish so the paint doesn't rub off.

EQUIPMENT
Jar of water   *Saucer*

You will need

Medium paintbrush

Thin paintbrush   *Poster paints*

Empty bottles or jars (plastic or glass)

Clear varnish

Craft glue

PAINTING THE BOTTLE

Make sure the bottle or jar is clean and dry. Mix a little craft glue with the paint. This helps the paint stick to the glass or plastic.

Paint a design on the bottle or jar. A simple idea is to dab on dots of paint all over the bottle. Try using lots of different colors.

When the paint is dry, paint clear varnish on the bottle or jar. This will protect the paint and give a shiny finish.

The finished bottles and jars
The finished jars and bottles make perfect vases, pencil holders, or brush pots, and are excellent gifts for friends and family.

A border around the rim adds the finishing touch.

Here, one color has been painted into another.

PAINTING TIPS
- Keep the paint fairly thick so that it doesn't run.
- If you make a mistake, wipe the paint off before it dries and start again.

You can cover the container completely, or leave some glass or plastic showing.

A simple pattern of zigzags, dots, and circles suits this narrow jar.

20

21

5

PAINTING KIT

Here you can see the tools and equipment that you need to paint the projects in this book. For most of the activities you can use poster paints, but for some you will need special paints, such as fabric or marbling paints, which you can buy in arts and crafts stores. Some of the projects are painted with sponges or nailbrushes; in others, pictures or patterns are scratched into paint with plastic knives or forks. Rags are useful for cleaning paintbrushes and other equipment, and you will need lots of newspaper to keep your work area clean.

Fabric paints

Newspaper

Marbling paints

Clear varnish protects paint and gives a glossy finish.

Poster paints

Acrylic paints usually come in tubes like this.

Acrylic paints

You can make more colors by mixing paints together. See pages 8–9 to find out how.

Old saucers make good painting palettes.

Ready-mixed, water-based paints

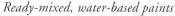

Ready-mixed, water-based paints often come in large squeeze bottles.

6

Thick paintbrush

Choose thin brushes with pointed ends to paint fine lines.

Medium paintbrush

Thin paintbrush

Rags

Flat brush

Paint large areas with a thick or flat-ended brush.

Stencil brush

Large, flat paintbrush or old pastry brush

Printing roller (You can buy these from art supply stores.)

Thin household sponges can be used for painting and to make printing pads.

Old nailbrush or scrub brush

Flour for thickening paint

Use an old cookie sheet and a sponge as a printing pad.

Craft glue for thickening paint and gluing things

Instead of a saucer, you could use a muffin pan as a palette.

Plastic knife and fork

7

MIXING COLORS

You can mix lots of different colors of paint
from just a few main colors. Follow this
step-by-step guide to color mixing to find
out how.

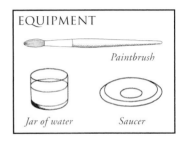
PRIMARY COLORS

*Red, yellow, and blue are called
primary colors. These colors,
along with white, cannot be
mixed from any other colors.*

SECONDARY COLORS

*Secondary colors can be made by mixing together
two primary colors. For example, green is made from
blue and yellow. Try mixing together different colors
of paint and make some colors of your own.*

Red

Red mixed with yellow makes...

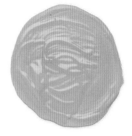

...orange

Blue

Blue mixed with red makes...

...purple

Yellow

Yellow mixed with blue makes...

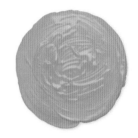

...green

LIGHT AND DARK

To make a color lighter, add some white paint. The more white you add, the lighter the color will be. To make a color darker, add a little black paint, or try another dark color.

Red and white makes...

...pink

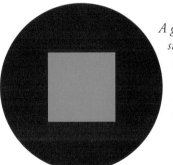

Red and black makes...

...dark red

COLOR WHEEL

The color wheel shows the three primary colors and the secondary colors you can mix from them. If you mix together a primary color and a secondary color, you get a tertiary color. For example, if you mix together blue and green, you get a dark blue-green.

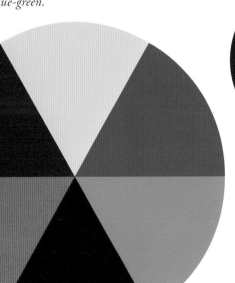

COMPLEMENTARY COLORS

Colors that are opposite each other on the color wheel are called complementary; they look very bright and exciting.

A green square stands out on a red background because green is a complementary color of red.

An orange square fades into a red background because the two colors are next to each other on the color wheel.

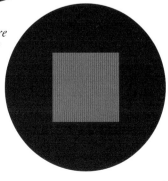

9

PERFECT PRINTS

Printing is a fun way to use paint and the results look great. Thick, sticky paint works best. All kinds of things such as cardboard, vegetables, or even your fingers can be used as printing tools. A sponge on an old cookie sheet makes a good printing pad. To keep from mixing colors, use one tool for each color and let the first color dry when printing one color over another.

EQUIPMENT

Sharp knife

Scissors

Cookie sheet

Household sponges

Jar of water

You will need

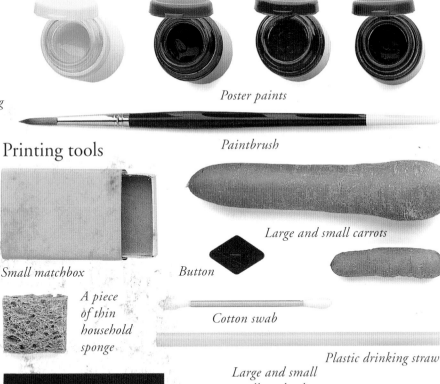

Writing paper

Poster paints

Paintbrush

Printing tools

Small matchbox

Large and small carrots

Button

A piece of thin household sponge

Cotton swab

Plastic drinking straw

Envelopes

Large and small cardboard tubes

Thick cardboard

Ridged cardboard

PRINTING THE PAPER

Put some damp sponges on an old cookie sheet. Pour paint and a little water on to the sponges*. Spread out the paint with a brush.

Ask an adult to cut the carrots. Cut a sponge shape. Press each tool into the paint and place firmly on paper to make a print**.

Print with different colors and tools to make a pattern or picture on the paper. Put more paint on each tool every few prints.

*The paint needs to be thick and sticky.
**Practice on scrap paper first.

The finished prints

Try printing a border, a stamp mark, or a picture on the paper and envelopes. Make sure you leave space to write in!

Ground printed with the edge of ridged cardboard

Tree prints made with sponge and the edge of cardboard

Circle print made with a cardboard tube

Pattern printed with a button and a small tube

Border printed with a triangular sponge

Circle prints made with a cotton swab and a straw

Tractor printed with carrots, a matchbox, the edge of cardboard, and a cotton swab

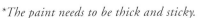

GIFT BAGS

You can learn to make printing blocks out of modeling clay and create fabulous patterned paper. Use thick paint, sponges, and an old cookie sheet, as on page 11. You can turn your printed paper into gift bags, or use the sheets as wrapping paper.

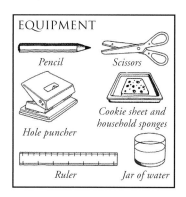

EQUIPMENT

Pencil

Scissors

Hole puncher

Cookie sheet and household sponges

Ruler

Jar of water

You will need

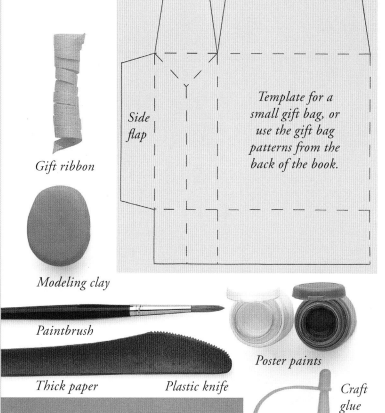

Gift ribbon

Modeling clay

Side flap

Template for a small gift bag, or use the gift bag patterns from the back of the book.

Paintbrush

Thick paper

Plastic knife

Poster paints

Craft glue

Tracing paper

MAKING THE GIFT BAG

Shape a lump of modeling clay. Flatten one side and make marks in it. Use different shaped lumps to make different prints*.

Press the clay into the printing pad. Then print a pattern on a sheet of paper. Let the paint dry before printing a new color.

Trace the template on to tracing paper with a pencil. Then color over the lines with the pencil, as shown.

Here, dots are made in a roll of clay and crossed lines are made in a round lump.

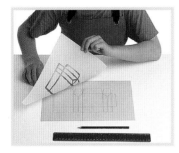

Turn over the tracing paper. Place it on the back of the dry printed sheet of paper. Draw over the template twice, as shown**.

Cut out the bag pattern. Score along all the lines and fold them, as shown, to make the bag. Glue the side flap and let it dry.

Glue the bottom flaps. You can put something heavy in the bag to help them to stick. When dry, punch two holes in the top.

The finished gift bags

Here are some ideas for patterns and colors to print on your bags. You can make different-sized bags by changing the size of the template, or cut out and use the patterns from the back of the book.

A diamond was marked into a square of clay to make the printing block for the blue diamonds.

The printing block for the circles was made by pressing a button into a round lump of clay.

For this block, the outline of a boat was marked into clay and then the whole boat was cut out.

Boats and waves

For the waves block, the outline of waves was marked into clay and then the clay around the outline was cut away.

GIFT TAGS

Cut out small rectangles from the paper and fold them to make tags. You can then cut the folded rectangles into other shapes, if you wish. Use a hole puncher to make a hole for the ribbon.

Flowers

Circles and diamonds

**Leave off he side flap the second time you draw over the lines of the template.

13

WONDERFUL WAX

Wax and paint do not mix, but they can be used together to create an exciting picture. Here, thick paint is painted over wax crayon and then scratched off to make a picture of colorful fireworks. Find out how to frame your picture on page 46.

frame your picture on page 46.

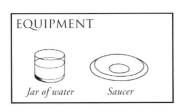

EQUIPMENT

Jar of water   *Saucer*

You will need

Black poster paint

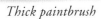

Ice-pop stick

Light-colored paper

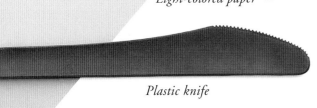

Plastic knife

Thin paintbrush

Thick paintbrush

Wax crayons

MAKING THE PICTURE

Use brightly colored wax crayons to draw a pattern on a sheet of paper. Fill the sheet of paper with the pattern.

Paint over the pattern with thick black paint. Make sure the pattern is completely covered. You may need two coats of paint.

When the paint is dry, draw a picture by scratching off the paint with a plastic knife, an ice-pop stick, or the end of a paintbrush.

The finished picture

When the black paint is scratched off, you can see the crayon underneath. Bright colors show up well, so use as many brightly colored crayons as you want to make the pattern.

You can find out how to scratch shapes into wet paint on page 44. The marks on the frame were made in this way.

You can use the ice-pop stick to scrape off large areas of paint.

The end of a paint-brush makes a medium mark.

Painted cardboard frame

Zigzags, swirls, and stars make brilliant exploding fireworks!

FRAME IT!

A frame adds the finishing touch to a picture. You can find out how to make picture frames on page 46.

Thin or thick marks can be scratched out with the plastic knife.

15

STENCIL DESIGNS

Stenciling is a fun way to repeat a picture or pattern. A stencil is a piece of cardboard with shapes cut out of it. To stencil, hold the cardboard flat on a surface and paint through the holes. Below, a palette and border of squares are stenciled on an art box. You can make up a picture or pattern to stencil. Leave a border of cardboard around your designs and varnish the stencils to make them last. You will need thick poster paints or acrylic paints and a stencil brush or sponge to paint with.

A piece of thin household sponge

You will need

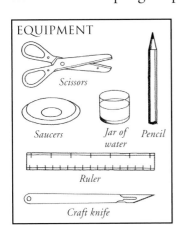

EQUIPMENT

Scissors

Saucers

Jar of water

Pencil

Ruler

Craft knife

Clear varnish

Paintbrush for varnishing the stencils

Stencil brush (or a brush with short, stiff hairs)

Poster paints (or you can use acrylic paints)

MAKING THE BOX

Cut two pieces of cardboard to fit the length of the box. Make them twice the depth of the box and fold them in half, as shown.

Paint or cover two matchboxes. Cut a length of cardboard to go across the box*. Make it twice the depth and fold in half, as before.

Cut a slit halfway down one long partition and another halfway up the short partition, so that they slot together, as shown.

The cardboard should fit across the box from one side to the matchboxes, as shown.

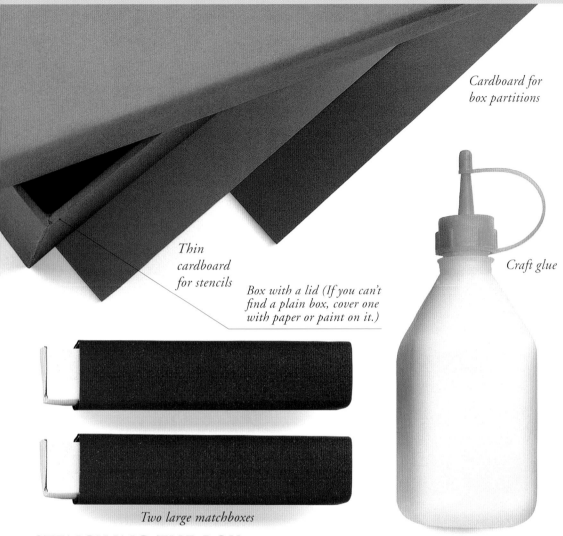

Cardboard for
box partitions

*Thin
cardboard
for stencils*

*Box with a lid (If you can't
find a plain box, cover one
with paper or paint on it.)*

Craft glue

Two large matchboxes

STENCILING THE BOX

Draw a pattern or picture on a piece of cardboard. Ask an adult to cut out your design. Varnish both sides. Leave to dry.

Decide where you want your design to go on the box. Hold the stencil flat**. Paint in the holes with a stencil brush or sponge.

You can use more than one stencil to make a picture or pattern. Wait for the first color to dry before stenciling over it.

**If you find it hard to hold the stencil in place, tape it down with masking tape.

STENCILED ART BOX

Your stenciled design can be repeated on each side of the art box, on the lid, and the matchboxes. You can fill the box with painting and drawing equipment. The bigger compartments can hold paintbrushes, paints, and pencils. The matchboxes are perfect for paper clips, erasers, or crayons. You might have room for items such as scissors, sponges, modeling tools and clay, and varnish. The box could also be used to store jewelry, sewing equipment, or a collection.

Matchboxes make small compartments. Use as many as you need.

The three partitions divide the box into large and small compartments, which can hold different-sized objects.

A PLACE FOR EVERYTHING

Before you cut out your partitions, put everything you want the art box to hold into the box. This will help you to decide on the best way to divide up your box.

STENCILING TIPS

* *You may find it easier to paint the outside edge of the stencil hole first and work inward.*

* *To keep from smudging the paint, don't take the stencil away until the paint is dry.*

* *Use thick, sticky paint so that it doesn't run under the stencil.*

The line of small red and yellow squares makes a decorative border.

Simple shapes
work well when
stenciled, such
as these squares.

PAINTING THEME
Two stencils were used for the palette design.
First, the palette was stenciled in white
and left to dry. Then the second stencil
was held over the palette and the
blobs of paint and brush were
stenciled on top.

White palette
stenciled first

Paints and
brush stenciled
over palette

19

PAINTED BOTTLES

Try turning empty bottles or jars into pretty vases and pots. Clean and dry the bottles or jars before painting them. Be careful with glass: keep the bottle or jar on a table while painting it. Finish with a coat of varnish so the paint doesn't rub off.

EQUIPMENT

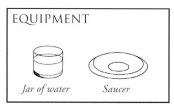

Jar of water   *Saucer*

You will need

Medium paintbrush

Thin paintbrush

Poster paints

Empty bottles or jars (plastic or glass)

Clear varnish

Craft glue

PAINTING THE BOTTLE

Make sure the bottle or jar is clean and dry. Mix a little craft glue with the paint. This helps the paint stick to the glass or plastic.

Paint a design on the bottle or jar. A simple idea is to dab on dots of paint all over the bottle. Try using lots of different colors.

When the paint is dry, paint clear varnish on the bottle or jar. This will protect the paint and give a shiny finish.

20

The finished bottles and jars
The finished jars and bottles make perfect vases, pencil holders, or brush pots, and are excellent gifts for friends and family.

A border around the rim adds the finishing touch.

Here, one color has been painted into another.

PAINTING TIPS
• Keep the paint fairly thick so that it doesn't run.
• If you make a mistake, wipe the paint off before it dries and start again.

You can cover the container completely, or leave some glass or plastic showing.

A simple pattern of zigzags, dots, and circles suits this narrow jar.

21

T-SHIRT PAINTING

Paint your own T-shirts and create unique patterns by splattering one color or more on to the fabric. Remember to lay down lots of newspaper when flicking paint in this way. You will need special fabric paints that can be bought from arts and crafts stores. Check the instructions that come with your paints. You may need to ask an adult to iron your T-shirt on the reverse side to fix the paint when it has dried. Turn the page to see the finished splattered T-shirt.

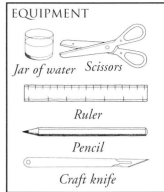

EQUIPMENT

Jar of water   Scissors

Ruler

Pencil

Craft knife

You will need

Masking tape

Fabric paints (Choose colors that will show up well on your T-shirt.)

Old nailbrush or scrub brush

T-shirt

SPLATTERING THE T-SHIRT

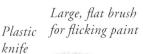

Plastic knife

Large, flat brush for flicking paint

Two sheets of corrugated cardboard (bigger than T-shirt)

Paintbrush

1. Push cardboard into the shirt to stop the paint from soaking through*. Tape the sleeves and bottom of the shirt, as shown.

2. Draw a square with 8 in (20 cm) sides in the center of a piece of cardboard. Ask an adult to cut out the square, leaving a frame.

3. Place the cut-out square in the middle of the front of the shirt and mark its position with tape. Then remove the square.

4. Line up the frame with the tape on the T-shirt and tape it down, as shown. Cover any parts of the T-shirt that still show.

5. Put fabric paint on a nailbrush. Use a plastic knife to flick the paint away from your body and on the shirt. Leave it to dry.

6. Dip a brush into a new color. Splatter the paint on to the T-shirt. When dry, ask an adult to iron the shirt to fix the paint**.

*Cut the cardboard to fit inside the T-shirt.

**First check the instructions that come with your paints.

23

DAZZLING DESIGNS

Here are three finished T-shirts plus some ideas for other things that you can decorate with fabric paints. Try painting a pair of socks or a baseball cap to match your T-shirt, or brighten up old handkerchiefs, pillow cases, tablecloths, or cotton scarves. In addition to splattering on fabric, you can print, stencil, or paint a picture with a brush. Turn to pages 10, 12, and 16 for instructions on printing and stenciling.

Printed daisy

FABRIC PAINTING TIPS

- *Ask an adult to iron the fabric first so that it is completely flat when you paint it.*
- *Always put a thick sheet of cardboard under the fabric because paint will soak through.*
- *The fabric will absorb a lot of paint so you may need two coats. Let the first coat dry before you paint the second.*

SPLATTERED SQUARE

Load your brush with paint and keep splattering and flicking until no more paint comes off. You can also make a splatter picture on paper. Turn to page 47 to see a framed splatter picture.

SOCKS TO MATCH

Try painting a pair of socks to match your T-shirt.

SPLATTER PATTERN

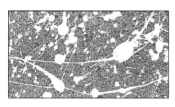

When you take away the frame and masking tape, you will be left with a neat splattered square. You can use triangular or round frames to make different shaped designs.

PRINTED DAISIES

You can splatter the back of the shirt as well as the front.

STENCILED CAR

Printed spots

Stenciled car

HANDKERCHIEF SPOTS
Turn a plain cotton handkerchief into a spotted one. A cotton swab was used to print these spots.

CAP
Try stenciling a design on the bill of a cap.

VEHICLE STENCILS
The white rectangles were sponged on first. Then the blue car and truck were stenciled on top. Turn to page 16 for instructions on stenciling.

DAISY PRINTS
Modeling clay was used to make the printing blocks for the daisies on this shirt (see page 12 for this technique). Chains of daisies have been printed across the front and back of the T-shirt and around the sleeves.

You can touch up any faint prints with a paintbrush.

PAINTED PEBBLES

Turn pebbles into colorful painted fish and create an amazing underwater world where they can swim! The pebbles hang in a shallow box on invisible thread. Look on the beach or in a park for different-sized pebbles or stones and fishlike shapes. Find pictures of tropical fish for ideas to paint them. Turn the page to see the finished seascape.

Seaside collection

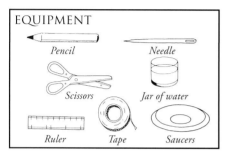

EQUIPMENT

Pencil

Needle

Scissors

Jar of water

Ruler

Tape

Saucers

You will need

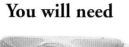

Clear varnish

Pebbles

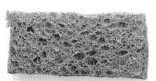

A piece of thin household sponge

Medium paintbrush

Thin paintbrush

Poster paints

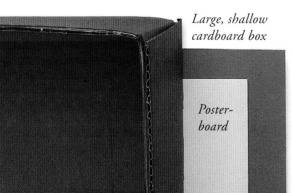

Large, shallow cardboard box

Poster-board

Paper

Craft glue

Invisible thread or clear fishing line

MAKING THE SEASCAPE

1. Paint or glue paper over any writing on your box to give it a neat finish. You may need two coats of paint to paint the box.

2. Paint a sandy seabed and an underwater background on the inside of the box. Try dabbing on paint with a sponge.

3. Draw sea plants and corals on posterboard and cut them out. Fold them over at the bottom so that they stand up.

4. Paint the plants and corals with a sponge. When dry, glue the flaps and stick them to the bottom of the box to make a scene.

5. Wash and dry the pebbles. Mix some white paint with craft glue and paint an undercoat on the pebbles. Leave them to dry.

6. Put the pebbles on a saucer so you can turn them without touching them. Use paints mixed with craft glue to paint the pebbles.

7. When the paint is dry, varnish the pebbles to protect the paint. When they are dry, tie a length of thread around each pebble*.

8. Ask an adult to use a needle to pull the lengths of thread through the top of the box, as shown**. Tape them down.

9. Arrange shells, driftwood, or stones on the base of the box. You can paint sea animals on more pebbles and add these as well.

*We have used black thread to show you what to do. You can use invisible thread.

**Hold the fish in place first to work out how many threads you need and where you want them to hang.

27

FISHY SCENE

You can keep the finished underwater scene on a table, bookshelf, or window sill. If you tap the box gently, all the fish will move, just as if they were swimming in the water!

SETTING THE SCENE
Wait for everything to dry before you assemble the scene. Hang the fish at different levels so that they fill the box.

PLANTS AND CORALS
You can add depth to the scene by positioning large sea plants and corals at the back and smaller ones in the middle and at the front of the box. The fish can swim in between the plants and corals.

SHOALS OF FISH
Fish often swim together in groups or "shoals." Here the orange, yellow, and blue fish have been arranged into groups.

In addition to fish, you can paint sea plants, crabs, or other sea creatures on stones.

Make a seaside collection of shells, stones, small rocks, or driftwood for the seabed.

You can leave some of the box showing to add texture to the scene.

28

The outside of the box has been covered with blue paper.

If the thread slips off the pebbles, use clear tape to hold it in place.

MIXING COLORS

Different shades of blue have been made for the background by mixing up different amounts of blue and white paint. The paint has been dabbed on with a sponge.

FABULOUS FISH!

The pebbles were painted in two stages. The base color was painted first. Once dry, eyes, fins, and scales were painted on top with a thin brush.

The plants and corals were painted by dabbing on orange, green, and white paint with a sponge. Try sponging one color over another.

29

A DIAMOND KITE

Make a colorful kite from a large plastic bag. Look for
a bag without any writing on it, such as a garbage
bag. Acrylic paints work best on plastic. You can
also mix a little craft glue with poster paint, but
you may find that some of the paint peels off
the plastic. Plant stakes are used for the kite
spars. They make a frame for the plastic using
medium-sized canes about 18 in (45 cm) long.

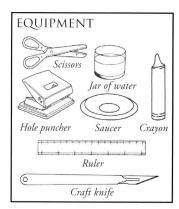

EQUIPMENT

Scissors

Jar of water

Hole puncher   *Saucer*   *Crayon*

Ruler

Craft knife

Strong adhesive tape

You will need

Thin paintbrush

Medium paintbrush

Small stick

*About 1 yd (90 cm)
of strong yarn*

*Large ball
of string*

Gift ribbon

Acrylic paints

*Plant
stakes*

*Large
plastic bag*

MAKING THE KITE

1. Cut a 19 in (48 cm) square from plastic. Make three marks 6 in (15 cm) from the top, and three along the center, as shown*.

2. Connect the marks on the plastic's edge. The plastic should be slightly bigger than the canes all around. Cut out the kite.

3. Tape the front and back of the kite: on the center line (4 in/11 cm from the top, 2.5 in/7 cm from the bottom) and corners.

4. Fold each corner and punch through the folds to make two holes. Ask an adult to cut two slits on the center line**.

5. Paint a design on the kite and leave to dry. Cut long lengths of gift ribbon. Hold them together and punch a hole in one end.

6. Turn over the kite. Thread one cane through the holes across the kite. Wrap tape over each end to hold the cane in place.

7. Thread the ribbons on to the other cane. Push it into the top and bottom boles, and under the first cane. Tape over the cane ends.

8. Turn over the kite. Push the ends of the yarn through the slits in the kite's center and tie them to the upright cane in the back.

9. Tie a small loop in the yarn. It should be at a right angle to the kite, as shown. This is the kite's bridle.

*Fold the plastic in half to find the center.

**Cut the slits through the tape pieces you placed on the center line in step 3.

FLYING DRAGON
ATTACHING THE STRING

Wrap tape around each end of a stick. Tie one end of a large ball of string to the stick and wind on about 100 ft (30 m) of string.

When you are ready to fly your kite, tie the end of the string to the loop in the bridle. Knot it two or three times.

LAUNCHING THE KITE

Find an open space. Unwind a little string. Stand with your back to the wind and hold the stick at each end. On a windy day, the kite should fly from your outstretched arm. Once your kite is up, slowly let out more string.

Pull on the string and watch your kite rise up into the air!

The finished kite

You can copy this face or paint a different face on your kite—try an octopus, a lion, or a monster.

DO'S AND DONT'S

- Never fly your kite in strong winds or stormy weather.
- Never fly near overhead cables, roads, cars, buildings, trees, people, animals, or an airport.
- Always wear gloves when kite-flying.

If your kite doesn't fly very well, try adjusting the angle of the loop in the bridle.

A long tail looks spectacular and keeps your kite steady. Red and gold ribbons suggest fire coming from the dragon's mouth.

The thick tape strengthens the plastic.

The ends of the yarn
are pushed through
the slits and tied to
the upright cane.

Make sure that the plant stakes
lie on the side of the kite that
isn't painted and that they hold
the plastic fairly taut.

33

MAKING A COLLAGE

Everyday things can be used in a collage. Make a collection of materials that you think would look interesting. You don't have to use the materials shown: dried pasta shells, grains of uncooked rice, sand, fabric, string, and magazine pictures are just a few more ideas. Below, a city scene is made with collage materials. Turn the page to see the finished picture.

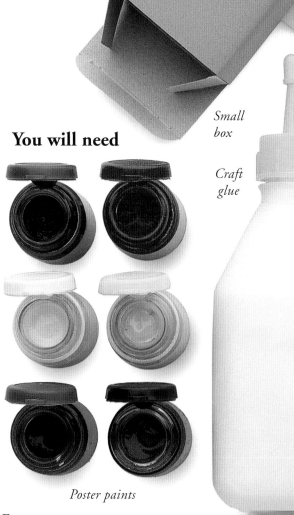

You will need

Small box

Craft glue

Poster paints

EQUIPMENT

Pencil

Jar of water

Scissors

Saucer

MAKING THE COLLAGE

Cut out and arrange your collage materials on cardboard to make a picture. Work out the main parts of your collage first.

When you are happy with your picture, glue the materials on the cardboard. Build up layers to make the collage stand out.

Different shapes and textures will add variety to your collage. Here, strips of corrugated cardbaord are used to make a pattern.

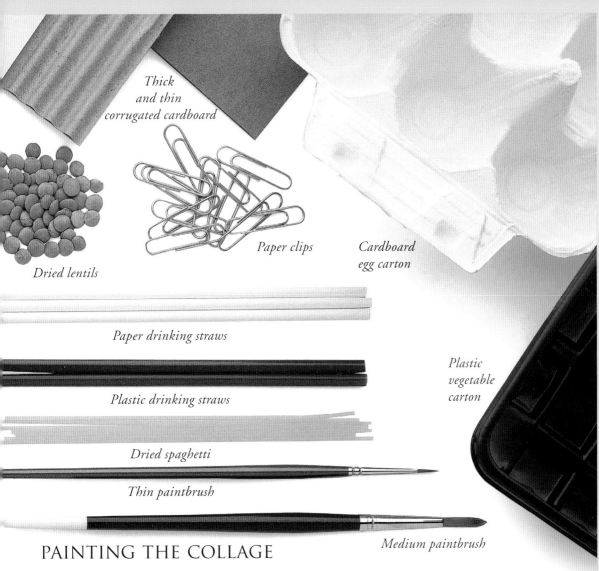

*Thick
and thin
corrugated cardboard*

Dried lentils

Paper clips

*Cardboard
egg carton*

Paper drinking straws

Plastic drinking straws

*Plastic
vegetable
carton*

Dried spaghetti

Thin paintbrush

Medium paintbrush

PAINTING THE COLLAGE

When the glue is dry, paint the collage. Mix each color with a little craft glue to help the paint coat the plastic materials*.

Paint the background. You can build up texture by adding more craft glue to the paint to thicken it.

Small things, such as paper clips or lentils, can be used to add detail. Stick them into the paint on the collage before it dries.

Mixing the paint with glue also allows you to stick small things right into the wet paint.

35

CITY SKYLINE

Here is the finished city scene. Tall buildings have been made from different types of cardboard and parts of a plastic vegetable carton. You can make a collage of anything you like: try a country scene, a picture of a farm, or the street where you live.

CARDBOARD BACK
Glue your materials on to thick cardboard. Paper won't be strong enough to hold them.

STICKY PAINT
You can stick small things into the wet paint if it has been mixed with craft glue.

Paper clips

Smaller buildings are stuck on to the taller buildings. This makes the taller buildings look as if they are in the distance.

Plastic veggie carton

Plastic straws and strips of corrugated cardboard make a door.

Paper clips, pasta, or legumes can be arranged into interesting patterns.

Paint has been thickened with craft glue to add texture to the cloudy sky.

Lentils

Dried spaghetti

Plastic carton

You can leave some parts of the collage unpainted.

Thin strips of corrugated cardboard form a crane.

CHOOSING COLORS

Think about the colors that you are going to use. Browns, grays, blues, oranges, and yellows have been mixed and used here to paint the stone, brick, concrete, and metallic buildings.

Part of a cardboard egg carton makes a perfect roof for this building.

Paper straws are used to make windows.

A FITTING FRAME!

The collage has been framed with corrugated cardboard. Learn how to make this frame on page 47.

Thin strips of corrugated card

Cardboard box

37

PINS AND BROOCHES

With some cardboard, papier-mâché, and poster paint, you can design and paint a pin in any shape you like: try making your favorite animal, machine, vehicle, a round face, a sun, or a moon. To make the papier-mâché mixture for the pins, you need to tear newspaper into tiny pieces and then mix the pieces with a little water and wallpaper paste. It should be a very smooth, doughlike mixture. Let your papier-mâché pins dry overnight before you start to paint them.

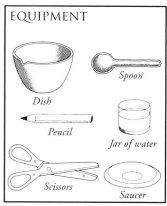

EQUIPMENT

Dish

Spoon

Pencil

Jar of water

Scissors

Saucer

You will need

Strong glue

Cardboard

Poster paints

Thin paintbrush

Medium paintbrush

Brooch safety pins

Clear varnish

A few sheets of newspaper

Thick wallpaper paste

21

38

MAKING THE PINS

Draw a shape on cardboard and cut it out. Tear newspaper into tiny pieces and mix with water and wallpaper paste in a dish.

Mash up the papier-mâché until it has the texture of dough. Put some on the cardboard. Shape it and leave it to dry overnight.

Paint a design on the pin front and paint the back in one color. Leave to dry. Glue the pin to the back. Varnish the pin.

The finished pins
A thin paintbrush will help you to paint detail on the small pins. Here are some different designs.

The varnish makes the pins stronger and gives a shiny finish.

Papier-mâché was built up to make the frame on this pin.

Here, papier-mâché has been shaped to look like fur.

Let one color dry before you paint the next.

Dinosaur

Boat

Dog

Sun face

Framed picture

Butterfly

Car

39

MARBLING PAPER

Try making beautiful marbled papers and then use them to cover a folder. To make a marble effect, special paints are dripped into water and form patterns on the surface. You then place paper on the water to pick up the paint. You may need to thicken the water with a special powder before you drip in the paint, so check the kit's instructions.

You will need

Ribbon

Posterboard sheets for folder (a bit smaller than the paper)

Craft glue

Plastic drinking straws

Thickening powder

Thick paper for inside of folder and flaps

Sheets of paper (smaller than the roasting pan) for marbling.

Strong, wide tape

Marbling paints (oil paints can also be used)

MARBLING THE PAPER

1. Fill an old roasting pan with about 1 in (2 cm) of water*. Use straws to drip a few drops of each paint color into the water.

2. Gently swirl the paint around with a straw to make a pattern in the water. Burst any bubbles on the surface with the straw.

3. Lay a sheet of paper on the surface of the water, holding it by opposite ends. Gently press down on the paper, as shown.

MAKING THE FOLDER

4. Lift up the paper and put it face up on a newspaper to dry. If you used thickening powder, rinse the wet paper under water.

1. You will need two sheets of marbled paper for a folder. Glue each sheet to some posterboard to make the two sides of the folder.

2. Ask an adult to cut a small slit in both sides of the folder. Push a length of ribbon through each slit and glue down, as shown.

3. Tape the two outer corners on both sides of the folder. Then glue a sheet of thick paper to the inside of both sides of the folder.

4. Line up the sides of the folder, leaving a 1 in (2 cm) gap between them. Connect them with two strips of tape. Make three flaps**.

5. Glue the flaps inside the folder on the right-hand side. There should be a tiny space between the flaps so they fold over easily.

*If using thickening powder, stir it into the water and leave to thicken, as instructed.

**Cut out and fold two flaps for the short edges of the folder and one for the long edge.

41

MARBLED FOLDERS

Choose tape and ribbon for your folder in colors that will go with your marbled papers. You can make different patterns every time. Experiment by swirling the paint in different directions, or leave it unswirled. You can also cover notebooks or diaries with your papers, use them as wrapping paper, gift bags and tags, or simply frame them as pictures.

Strong, wide tape around corners

Ribbon

Strong, wide tape on spine of folder

MARBLING TIPS
- *Make sure the paper you use is flat.*
- *Before you lay the paper on the water's surface, burst any bubbles in the water.*
- *Lightly rest your fingers on the paper when it is on the water to remove any remaining bubbles.*
- *You can make many sheets of marbled paper with the same water.*

The two strips of tape joining the two sides of the folder together make a flexible spine.

The three flaps hold your paper or picture in the folder.

Stick the flaps a little way in from the edge of the folder.

Thick paper is used to make the flaps.

SCRATCH AND SCRAPE

Try scraping marks into thick paint to make a textured painting. You can scratch out all kinds of different patterns. Use flour to thicken ready-mixed, water-based paints. Make sure that the flour is thoroughly mixed into the paint. When painting the picture, work quickly, or the paint will dry before you can scrape it!

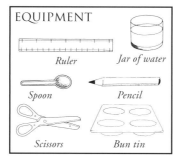

Ruler   Jar of water

Spoon   Pencil

Scissors   Bun tin

You will need

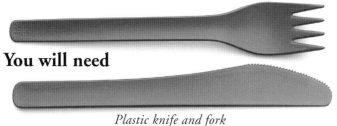

Plastic knife and fork

Paintbrush

Posterboard

Ready-mixed, water-based paints

Flour

Craft glue

MAKING THE PICTURE

Cut out a sheet of posterboard for the background. Draw shapes on another sheet*. Mix a little flour into each paint color.

Paint the background. Scrape different patterns into the paint with a plastic knife and fork. Do the same with the shapes.

When the shapes are dry, cut them out, arrange them into a design, and glue them to the dry background.

Work out what shapes you will need for your pattern on scrap paper first.

The finished picture
Here, diamonds and strips of posterboard are arranged to make a colorful pattern.

Diamonds

Strips of color

You can fit your shapes together like a jigsaw.

White mount

You can scrape swirls, straight lines, and different shapes into the paint.

This pattern was scraped with the teeth of a fork.

PAPIER-MÂCHÉ FRAME
Turn the page to find out how to mount and frame the picture.

FUN FRAMES

Frame your favorite paintings and hang them up at home. Below, you can find out how to make picture frames and make a "mount" (a border that surrounds a picture). You don't have to use a mount, but it can help a picture to stand out.

You will need

Corrugated cardboard

Thick posterboard

Paintbrush

Papier-mâché

Poster paints

Strong yarn

Craft glue

Adhesive tape

DOUBLE CARD-BOARD FRAME

Draw a rectangle on cardboard slightly bigger all around than the picture you want to frame*. Ask an adult to cut it out to make a frame.

Ask an adult to cut out a narrower frame to fit over the first frame, as shown. Glue the frames together and leave to dry.

Paint the frame. Try printing, splattering, or scratching the paint. Tape the frame to some cardboard so that it dries flat.

If your picture is square or round, draw a square or circle on the cardboard.

Mounting the picture

Glue your picture to posterboard the same size as the frame. Glue the frame to the posterboard and tape yarn to the back.

Papier-mâché frame

Ask an adult to cut out a single cardboard frame. Then thicken the frame with papier-mâché**. Let it dry overnight and paint it.

Corrugated frame

Cut out strips of corrugated cardboard and glue them to a single frame, as shown. When the glue is dry, paint the frame.

The frames
Paint your frame and choose a mounting card in a color to suit the picture you are framing. Look at the frames on this page and on pages 36, 45, and 48 for some ideas.

Corrugated frame

Papier-mâché frame

Double frame
Turn the page to see a printed double frame.

Scratched paint (see page 44 for this technique)

Splatter picture (see page 23 for splattering)

The white poster-board mount brings out the white in the splatter pattern.

FRAMING TIPS
* *Make sure your picture is in the center of the frame.*
* *You can make the frame wide or narrow. Choose a width to suit your picture.*
* *If you are not using a mount, the frame hole must be slightly smaller than your picture.*

**Turn to page 39 for instructions on making papier-mâché.

PAINTING TIPS

Practice on scrap paper first to work out
your picture, pattern, or design.

•

If you make a mistake, leave the paint
to dry and then paint over it.

•

When painting on construction paper,
tape your picture to thick cardboard to
stop it from curling up as the paint dries.

•

Change your brush water regularly and
have a rag handy for wiping brushes.

•

Always put the lids back on your paints
to stop them from drying out or spilling.

•

Work near a sink so that you can clean
up easily.

•

Clean brushes thoroughly with soapy
water. Ask an adult to help you use
paint thinner to clean brushes after using
oil-based varnish.

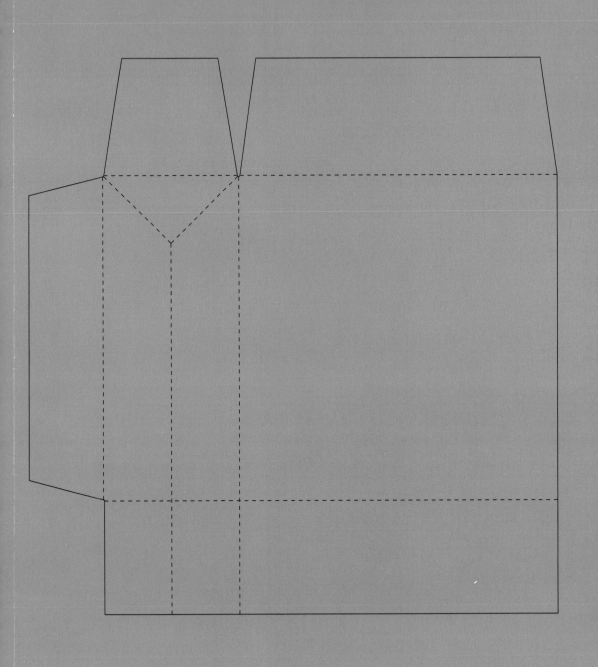